Y0-CAE-153

Crossing Jordan

RENEE CARLISLE

ISBN 978-1-64300-108-1 (Paperback)
ISBN 978-1-64300-109-8 (Digital)

Copyright © 2018 Renee Carlisle
All rights reserved
First Edition

All rights reserved. No part of this publication may be reproduced, distributed, or transmitted in any form or by any means, including photocopying, recording, or other electronic or mechanical methods without the prior written permission of the publisher. For permission requests, solicit the publisher via the address below.

Covenant Books, Inc.
11661 Hwy 707
Murrells Inlet, SC 29576
www.covenantbooks.com

INTRODUCTION

IN EVERY GOOD FAIRY tale, there is the trapped princess in the tower who is waiting for her knight in shining armor to come to her rescue. Then there is always the dragon that must be slain. And let's not forget how the princess ends up in the tower in the first place. There is always a story, and usually, betrayal is in there somewhere. This is true in this story.

This book has it all!

The princess: She was trapped in religion and a slave to sin, high in a tower of walls she built around her heart. She was deep in shame, condemnation, and guilt.

The villain: A nasty enemy who wants nothing more than to destroy the princess. He had her beauty and her position of authority in Christ and threw it all away because he was prideful and felt God was holding out on him. He does not want anyone else to get what he gave up. His whole purpose is not just to steal the princess' identity but also destroy her heart. Sound familiar? You may recall the story of the huntsman who took the princess deep into the woods after being instructed by a wicked, jealous queen to cut out her heart. This is to prove to the wicked queen that she is dead. This is the plot of the villain. He goes straight for the heart of the princess.

All is not lost!

The hero: He is the knight in shining armor who knows the heart of the princess, and he too will stop at nothing to win her heart. He will win her heart with love.

This is the struggle—the blood, sweat, and tears—of a girl born into religion but desperately searching for freedom. She leans over the high walls of the tower to see what lies beyond it. The hero, her Lord and Savior, sees this and knows it is time. It is time to scale the walls of her heart, and thus begins the journey of crossing over from religion to relationship and then there is the rescue of her heart!

Hang on to your seats! It is a bumpy ride!

CHAPTER 1

IN THE BEGINNING

ONCE UPON A TIME, there was a little girl who lived in a castle with her mom, dad, and siblings. She was the youngest of the children, and for the most part, she was protected. The king and queen of the castle were very busy, so oftentimes, other people were in charge of the children and the castle's care. The king and queen devoted their lives to the community around them, and it would seem to all who knew them that life was grand in the castle, but we know this is not that kind of story.

*****

The villain came early for me. This is no exception for most people. It is what Satan is known for. He strikes early. As soon as Satan sees there is life, it begins. I grew up in a very religious family. I often joke I came out of the womb reading the King James Version of the Bible. I was drenched in doctrine and religion. I was a church brat. Other kids played house, hide-and-seek, and tag. My siblings and I played church. One of us was the preacher, one was the deacon, and of course we drafted the neighborhood kids and they were the congregation. I ate, slept, and breathed church. I knew nothing else.

My parents were pastors of a fundamentalist Pentecostal church. My dad was kind of a pioneer pastor. He would move us to a town. He would start a Bible study in our home and then it would grow into a church plant. My parents did this several times in my childhood and youth. We moved a lot. I was the new girl, and I was always in a new place. We never really put down roots anywhere. I did not know the reason for this when I was little. In my adulthood, looking back, it is pretty obvious there was a reason for this. We had to move. My dad made choices that impacted our family in a very negative way.

One day, I came home from school, and my older sister was standing on the steps waiting for me. "Dad is gone," she said. My dad was pastoring a little church in a rural part of Indiana. He had left my mom and us kids and decided to take a young girl from the congregation with him. She was eighteen years old. She was homeless, and my mother moved her into our home. He not only left but also took all the church's money, all of our family's money, and the only vehicle we had. It's a tragic story, right? The enemy came very early for me. You can imagine the wounds this caused. It is a betrayal—a betrayal to my mother and siblings—and it was a betrayal to all the people he led to Christ. He was a broken man. His brokenness became our brokenness. His shame, we carried. It forever changed our family. My mother, although she has forgiven him, has never been the same. Years of marital issues and wounds festered like a blister underneath the surface of their relationship.

So you have a missing father, a very wounded mother, and children who were dealing with rejection, shame, loss, guilt, and whatever else the villain can throw at them. This was the household I grew up in. We moved to get away from shame. This attack on my family is nothing new. The enemy came for my family just like he does for every family. He strikes early before we have a chance to really know who we are and the power and authority we have in Christ. So most of us walk with a spiritual limp from the wounding. We limp around for years until we encounter the only one who can heal us, restore us, and set us free. It is just like the little girl in the castle. Once the enemy has invaded the castle, she goes into hiding. This is what I did for years.

In the Bible, there is a story of a young man named Mephibosheth. He is the son of Jonathan. I like to call him Fibby. You can read about it in Second Samuel chapter 9. He was the only relative who survived in King Saul's household after it was attacked by David and his men. As the story goes, the men were storming the castle. There should have been no survivors. No one should have been left to take the throne after King Saul was overthrown, especially not a son and a rightful heir. There was a nursemaid who cared for little Fibby. She picked him up during battle, and in her haste to escape with him, she dropped him and little Fibby who was already born crippled became even more so. From that day forward, he was permanently maimed.

So little Fibby hid in a place called LoDebar. I like to call it below the bar because it was definitely below the castle life he was born into. He was taken there and hid in his crippled state for the rest of his childhood and into adulthood. He was hiding in fear that if his identity was known, he would be killed. One day, King David remembered the covenant he made with his best friend Jonathan. He promised to Jonathan to always be there for him and his family. King David asked, "Is there anyone still left of the house of Saul to whom I can show kindness for Jonathan's sake?"

So there was a servant of Saul's household named Ziba who remembered Fibby was indeed alive. He told this to King David, and David sent for Fibby. Fibby came before the king, and he was terrified. It was heart wrenching! King David told him not to be afraid.

> "Don't be afraid," David said to him, "for I will surely show you kindness for the sake of your father Jonathan. I will restore to you all the land that belonged to your grandfather Saul, and you will always eat at my table." Mephibosheth bowed down and said, "What is your servant, that you should notice a dead dog like me?" (2 Sam. 9:7–8)

There it was! He didn't know who he was. The enemy came early for him, and he walked with a limp in a wasteland, not knowing he had the power and authority to be in David's household. He was hiding. We will come back to this story because this story has a powerful meaning to my story.

So in the beginning… is where it all starts. Satan came early for me, convincing me I was the reason my dad left. Maybe we were too loud as kids or caused too much trouble. The brokenness played out in most of my life and in the lives of my family members.

You see, if Satan, the villain in the story, can convince you that you have no worth or value, you will be powerless to take your place at the King's table just like Fibby. I call him Fibby because he swallowed a huge lie. He addressed himself, "A dead dog like me." Wow! What a low self-image Fibby had all because he was wounded so young. His household was overthrown, and he was dropped in the escape. Crippled from the experience, this guy had no idea what was actually his inheritance until the covenant from David was honored.

This is definitely a story I relate to. As long as we stay in our wounds and believe the lie that we have no worth or value, we are no threat to the villain. The minute we begin to see ourselves the way we were meant to see ourselves, we become full of life, and Satan hates life.

Why? We must go back to…

In the beginning, in the Garden of Eden, there was Adam and Eve, full of life, placed there by God to guard and keep the garden. Which of the two could actually one day bring forth life from their womb? That's right; it was Eve. Satan is very cunning. This is why he came to her first. He tricked her, and she believed the lie that somehow God had withheld from her and Adam. He did not give them the best. Lies! All of it was a lie! We fall for this too. It's an age-old trick our enemy, the deceiver, has used from the very beginning and will continue to use. It is what caused Satan to fall from heaven. He wanted the glory and power. He believed God was withholding from him. He fell, and he took others with him. This is what the fight is all about. It is about us taking our rightful place. It is the very place Satan gave up. He does not want us to have it. So the battle for our heart is on! Our heart is what brings life to us. It is what pumps the blood of passion through our veins and causes us to thrive. If our heart is fully alive and connected to Christ, whatever our passions and desires are, life will flow out of it. Good will happen. Restoration will come. Healing will come. Deliverance will come!

So this is what the fight is all about. Satan does not want us to take our rightful place and reign and rule with Christ here on this earth. We as believers are called to reign here with Christ, doing His work until He comes. Satan hates this. So we live in a fallen world where he temporarily has power because of sin. He uses this to keep people bound in shame and sin so we will not be used by God to further the kingdom of Heaven. God sees this and has made a covenant through the shedding of the blood of His son Jesus, the hero of the story, and He fights alongside us for our salvation, our healing, and ultimately our freedom from the past and our heart.

How do we get past the past? That is why I am sharing my story with you. If you are reading this and you are looking at yourself and the wounds, hurt, and scars from the spiritual crippling from your past, know God is a good God. He will come for your heart. He is a God who restores. He truly is the hero. In His great love and compassion for us, He does not want us to stay in captivity to our past. He longs to restore. It is a process. Freedom happens every day that you walk with God. It is a journey with purpose. The fight for our hearts is something we must engage in. There is no such thing as drive-through breakthrough. We have to engage in this thing called life with God. He is so good and so relational that He wants us to join Him in the restoration of our story. Every wound, one by one, He wants to heal. He then wants our story to be shared to help someone else who needs healing. He gets all the glory. This takes time. It is a process. The thing I have learned from my hero is He is not worried about the process. He sees the end result. He knows my heart. He comes for me when He knows I can handle it. He peels back another layer when I am ready. He does all of this with the cross and resurrection in mind. It was hard for me in the beginning to wrap my head around this, but Jesus, the hero of our story, looks at us and our hearts from a view of the cross. He really does see us as the righteousness of Christ and the finished work of the cross.

This blows my mind a little. I live with myself and all of my mess, and He loves me and all of my mess. So the hero gets the glory in my story. Will He in yours? I hope so. Whatever you have gone through up to this point, you need to remember this: you are still here, so there is purpose for your life. God wants to be the hero for you. He wants to come in and save the day for you. He already has through His son Jesus on the cross, but He is a personal and relational God. He wants to take the story of redemption and make it personal to you. I know He is a powerful God who could take away suffering just like that, but I believe there is purpose in the pain. He wants us to fight for our hearts. He is with us, waging war against the enemy of our souls, but He is relational and He wants us to walk it out. He does not bring on our pain, but He does work it for our good. This is what it looks like to reign with Christ here on earth. We will reign with Him in heaven forever, but make no mistake, the reigning starts here. Taking dominion starts here. In the beginning, He gave Adam and Eve dominion over every living thing. We still have that with Christ.

We will talk about our authority in Christ more later on, but for now, let me just say this: we were created for so much more than what most of us are aware of. Satan, the villain, knows exactly what we are capable of in Christ, and he is on a mission to destroy us before we ever get our feet wet. If he can destroy our hearts, he will. Out of our hearts, our life flows. Our desires, passions, dreams, and visions come from the heart. The snare of the enemy is to keep us going around and around the same old stump until we are worn out, distracted, and it feels like there is no hope. If we are wandering aimlessly, then we are not effective for the kingdom, but the more urgent thing is we are bleeding internally. Most of us don't even recognize it. Our hearts are so wounded that we can't see a way out. We just follow the path we have always followed and hope for a different outcome. That, my friends, is a good definition of insanity: doing the same thing over and over again and hoping for a different result. We get comfortable in our wounds, and for a lot of us, our wounds are normal. We don't really know anything else. This was my life. To this day, I still have to fight the urge to go back to those places of brokenness. It is a choice every day to ask the Holy Spirit to help me live as He wants me to live.

CHAPTER 2

✦

WOUNDS AND WANDERINGS

As SHE LEANS OVER the high walls of the castle, the princess begins to notice a world beyond the walls of the castle and life happening all around her. She begins to dream and wonder what it would be like to step outside her everyday surroundings and the safety of all she has ever known into a world unknown. There is a desire and a longing like the slight tug or pulling of a string that is attached to her heart. She just can't shake the feeling that there is more to life than what she has been told. The longing and tugging on her heartstrings never goes away.

*****

Growing up in my house was interesting to say the least. Change was a bad thing. Every time change came, it was because of something negative that had occurred in my life. We moved often. There was so much spiritual abuse in the church organization we were involved in. I now understand I was raised in a very cultish environment. Every decision my parents made, whether it was to move or buy a car or house or whatever, it went through the leader of the organization. Their leader and a prayer committee would make major decisions about my family's personal life. This was such an abuse. When my parents had marriage problems, a real counselor never counseled my dad. He had some major wounds from his childhood—wounds he should have been able to talk about with someone and get some real help so he could be the father he was meant to be.

This was so sad for me because my father is a great man. He loves God. He lives with so much regret. He needed help. He made poor choices out of his broken state. I am not making excuses for him, but clearly he needed help. He did not need to be placed in another church to pastor another congregation only to fail again. He was broken and never given the opportunity to heal until, one day, he made the decision for himself to resign from ministry, and even then he didn't get help. He was just defeated and threw in the towel. It was so sad for me as a young girl to watch him and my mother struggle after years of serving in the church. They were penniless and had to take jobs, doing whatever they could to support the family. This left my siblings and me alone for much of the time. There are so many stories I could tell, but I would rather share the process of how God came for me.

The first step to getting free is seeing there is a need for change. For most people who grew up like me in a very sheltered yet dysfunctional way, you trot along, not realizing there is a better way. It is all you know. I never knew the life I was living was one of brokenness. It was all I knew. So until you join your dysfunction to someone else, you don't have a clue. This brings me to the next step in my life: marriage. I married a wonderful guy. We have been together for twenty-five years. The thing is, he grew up in the same religion as I. His family life was nothing like mine. Other than being in a very legalistic cultish church setting, he was normal. For the first ten years we were married, we stayed in the church we were raised in. The brokenness began to show up in our life. Little by little, our eyes began to open to the unhealthy way we were living. We were faithful to the church and involved in everything. The dysfunction continued until, one day, we had enough and began to pray and ask God to show us a better way. There it began. When you are heavily drenched in doctrine and religion and spiritual abuse, it is a real process to get out of. Some people don't ever recover. It wasn't just doctrine and religion. There was such spiritual abuse and control going on—fear-based religion.

So my husband and I began to question the doctrine and, as the Bible says, judge the fruit of the church organization we grew up in. We finally made the decision to take a step back, really study the Bible for ourselves, and see whether how we were taught and what the Word of God says were the same. We began to slowly but surely open our eyes to the truth. This was quite a process. We ended up making the decision to leave the church of our youth.

The first year we were at our new church, we were healing and deprogramming. We did not participate in much. We sat on the sidelines, feeling very lost and disconnected from church, but we began to feel more connected with our faith in Christ. So the wanderings and the uncovering of the wounds began. Wandering around in very dry places, this is where people tend to give up. The condemnation and the voice of the accuser, the villain, was so strong, and we were wandering about, trying to piece our lives back together. Discovering everything you thought to be true is not true and realizing your whole identity is wrapped up in a lie is staggering. I can remember feeling very lost, yet I knew I had to keep going. I knew the hero was there. He was gentle and patient with me as He still is today.

There were mindsets I had that were very unhealthy. They kept me in my wounds for a very long time. So even though the prison gate had opened, I was still not free. I believed God loved me, but I still struggled and wandered without purpose for a good while after leaving the church of my childhood. It is so much like the princess trapped in the tower who gets rescued but doesn't really see she is actually free and doesn't know how to act with all the new freedom she has. The scheme of the enemy is to keep her in bondage and keep the wounds and unhealthy mindsets present and fresh, reminding her of her failures and the past mistakes she has made and offenses that has happened to her as well. I know there has to be people out there who can relate to this. Even though you came from dysfunction, it is familiar and it is your story, and it is really hard to walk away from. You are not just walking away from the dysfunction but also relationships and sometimes family members and lifelong friendships. So it is almost easier to just live in the dysfunction. But, my friends, once you get over the walls of the tower and begin to experience just a little bit of the freedom God has for you, it is worth it all. It is just taking that initial step to freedom and then Jesus is right there.

Loosed but Not Free

Even after swinging over the tower walls and meeting Jesus right where I was, there were some things I had to push through. I still do. I had some very unhealthy mindsets that were a hindrance to my freedom. You can be physically free, removed from a situation, but mentally trapped. Maybe you can relate.

Here are some unhealthy mindsets that kept me in my wanderings and wounds:

• I was better off where I was.

Oh boy! I can think of some people in the Bible who went through this very thing. In Exodus chapter 15–16, Pharaoh, the leader of Egypt, held the children of Israel captive, and they were in slavery. God rescued them from the hands of the Egyptians. He parted the Red Sea. God brought them out and performed miraculous wonders for them.

Then we read in chapter 16 that after going a few days in discomfort, the children of Israel began to murmur and complain and long for the way things used to be. They wanted to go back to slavery and bondage because at least then they would know what was expected of them and have nourishment. They were in fear and needed to trust God for their lives. The same God who parted the waters for them, brought them out of bondage, and destroyed their enemy, they did not trust. He then provided manna for them. They were not in a place to receive. This was my life for a very long time. After leaving and breaking away from the dysfunction, I still had no idea I was really free. This kept me wandering around aimlessly for a while. The familiar is what we long for even if it is unhealthy.

There is also something in all of us that comes out when we have been wronged. We want justice. This is dangerous because it causes us to focus on the wounds in our lives and the wrongdoings of others toward us and then comes the martyr role. I was so comfortable in my wounds I actually liked it there. It gave me an excuse to be angry. I felt justified. This is a very unhealthy way to live. It is an unhealthy mindset and perspective. I have so many relatives and friends who have been raised in the same church setting who ended up in really bad shape because they couldn't function outside the dysfunction. Their safety was in the rules and regulations. They were either in church and all in, or they were on drugs and medication. I have had family members die premature deaths due to their inability to function outside the religious walls of their youth. This is so sad to me. They would break away and try to get free and really could not recover. Church or drugs were the two bookends to the dysfunction they lived, and they would swing from one end to the other.

The process God took me through and is still taking me through is worth it. There were times when God felt silent. He was quietly guiding me, but I wanted Him to just make me whole. I wanted to wake up one day and just be normal. I could laugh at that now. Who is normal? What is the norm? Everyone has a story and has had things happen to them that cause them to question if they are normal. I have come to know I am not normal. I am extraordinary! You are too! In the quiet times, when I was trying to find my way and learning how to let God lead me, if I did not hear from Him, I would begin to doubt the decisions I had made to be free. Our walk to freedom is a walk of faith, not feelings. Feelings lie.

• Nothing has changed, so God must have changed His mind.

Once God has parted the Red Sea in our lives and we taste victory for a moment, we want to live out of that feeling and moment. I can remember the freedom I initially felt when I finally broke away and started my journey to freedom. It was exhilarating at first. Then after this, the condemnation and the real warfare from the enemy came. See, as long as you are already in bondage and not doing anything to get out of it, he leaves you alone. As soon as you choose to live in victory and begin making strides toward a life of wholeness, you become a threat to the enemy. He is relentless! We have to be relentless too. So when I started feeling the heat from the enemy, not realizing the warfare I was in, I thought I made a mistake. Maybe I should just turn back around and go back. Maybe God has changed His mind. Maybe He doesn't want me to do this. Otherwise I would feel better than I am feeling right now. This is a lie from the pit of hell. It is warfare. The enemy knows once you become free, you will walk in that freedom and go after others who need to be free as well. We pose a great threat to the enemy when we live in victory. Others will see Jesus in us, and they will want it too. They will sense His presence in your life.

Someone said, "Show me your wounds, and I will show you your calling." Out of our wounds, we can bring hope and healing to others. The devil knows if he can keep you focused on the past, he will hold your future up. He is more worried about what you will do, not what you have done. So then he will torment you with the thought that you are going to mess up so bad God will just be done with you. The enemy's strategy is to come after your very identity. You and I have a specific call and role in life. We bring something to the table no one else can bring. Our story, our journey, our life experiences are ours to share. He wants to shut us up. How does he do this? This leads me to my next mindset.

• I will miss God.

This one is a doozy. Because I had the wrong image of my heavenly Father, I thought for sure I was going to mess up. I was going to do something that was crossing the line. When you live a life of rules, regulations, and religion, you always know where the line is. After breaking free from all that and having an encounter with God and His grace, I would still question and wonder if I was going to mess up. I had no idea all was mine in Christ. The fear of missing God was very real for me. To this day, I still have to remind myself of His grace daily. I had no idea who I was. I had no identity, and I surely had the wrong impression of my heavenly Father. So I continued to wander. Until I read a verse in the Bible in Psalm chapter 139.

> O LORD, you have searched me and you know me. You know when I sit and when I rise; you perceive my thoughts from afar. You discern my going out and my lying down; you are familiar with all of my ways. Before a word is on my tongue you know it completely, O LORD. You hem me in—behind me and before; you have laid your hand upon me. (Pss. 139:1–5, NIV)

So while reading this, I began to get a picture of God all around me, hemming me in and then also laying His hand on me. He is so close to me that I am not going to miss Him! I would have to run from Him to get away! But then I kept reading, and verses 7–10 of Psalm chapter 139 says, "Where can I go from your spirit? Where can I go from your presence? If I go up to the heavens, you are there; if I make my bed in the depths, you are there. If I rise on the wings of the dawn, if I settle on the far side of the sea, even there your hand will guide me; your right hand will hold me fast."

So God is guiding us always! We will not miss Him. If we do, He is there to guide us back. So I had to remind myself that God has got me covered on every side. Again, it is by faith that we walk in freedom. Don't look at your struggles or the things that feel too big to overcome. Just keep walking.

• The giants in the land are too big!

I began to learn little by little about God and about being in Christ. I began to discover some things that were crucial to my healing. The first time I heard the statement "in Christ," I was in North Dakota. My husband is a medical device rep, and we were transplanted temporarily to Grand Forks, North Dakota. The pastor of the church we attended there used the phrase "in Christ." It was like a foreign language to me. I heard the words but had no idea what it meant. So I began to learn about our inheritance in Christ. I don't have a more tasteful way to say this; it was like a herd of cows that discovered a break in the fence. They are grazing in the field and then suddenly discovered the fence is broken. Do we dare go beyond the fence? I looked out at the pasture. I saw the land. I heard the words "in Christ." I began to experience joy I had never experienced before. I began to truly live. My heart came to life! With this new freedom came awareness to the land and its inhabitants.

I saw the giants in the land. They were huge. I knew there were some major obstacles in my life I was going to have to face, and they were gigantic. So the wandering around the edges of freedom happened for a season because I had the mindset that the giants in the land were too big!

It took some time to face the giants, so this left me on the outside for a while. God was still at work even then. He knew I was going to need time. God is not afraid of process. We are the ones who put time limits and restraints on God. We put Him in a box. We let Him in a little bit but not all the way. What we see overwhelms us. God is not moved or motivated by the giants in the land. He is there, and as many times as we need it, God is faithful to redirect us. He is a good God!

So while writing this book, I came across a scripture that makes my reference to cows finding a break in the fence all the more real to me.

> But unto you who revere and worshipfully fear My name shall the Sun of Righteousness arise with healing in his wings and His beams, and you shall go forth and gambol like calves (released) from the stall and leap for joy. (Mal. 4:2, AMP)

This made me smile. We are free in Christ!

CHAPTER 3

ON THE OUTSIDE LOOKING IN

SHE IS LOOKING AT the beautiful land in front of her. There is just one problem. It is gated. There are heavy iron gates around the land. How does she get in? For days, she stands at the portal and looks in. Her face is pressed up to the gate. She can see people. They are joyful. She can hear music and laughter. She can smell the wonderful smell of food. She can smell the flowers. She is so close she can even pick the bloom of a beautiful lavender flower sticking through the gate. She does it. She has the fragrant bloom up close to her face and then, all of the sudden, it wilts. It begins to turn gray and brown, and she drops it and it falls to the ground. What has caused this awful transformation to happen before her very eyes? She feels a hot breath on her neck. She turns and there is—yep, you guessed it—the villain. He kills anything not attached to life. He breathes death, vile and smelly. The beautiful bloom dies. The princess is discouraged. She almost turns completely around. Wait! The hero is there in one swooping motion, and the villain slowly fades out of sight... for now. Her hero says to her, "I am the true vine, and my Father is the gardener. He cuts off every branch in me that bears no fruit, while every branch that does bear fruit He prunes so it will be even more fruitful. He also says, 'Remain in me, and I will remain in you.' No branch can bear fruit by itself; it must remain on the vine." The princess then understands why the beautiful bloom withered. It was no longer attached to life. Thus one breath of death caused it to dry up and wither away. She hides this truth in her heart. She understands she too must stay close to her hero.

*****

As I stated in the previous chapter, my husband and I moved to Grand Forks, North Dakota. We actually had friends ask us if we were in the witness protection program. People couldn't believe we would go from Southeast Missouri, where we had lived all of our married life, to Grand Forks, North Dakota. It was an adventure for us. We have two beautiful children who, at that time, were in grade school. We moved our family there and joined a small church there. We loved it. This church had a Bible school that was held at the church. My husband and I joined. It was the best decision we have ever made. For so long after breaking away from religion and law and trying to receive God's grace, I still struggled. I can totally see why most people just walk away. God had a hold of me. That is my only explanation for why I am still here. He kept His hand on me. I believe with all my heart He orchestrated the move to North Dakota. He kept us there only one year before things fell apart with my husband's territory there, and we were relocated. That year was critical for me. I was in boot camp, spiritually speaking. I learned so much about the Word of God. For every lie I had swallowed, God brought truth. When we were relocated to Traverse City, Michigan, I was still like the cow that had wandered to the broken place in the fence, but I had vision for the first time. It was all in theory, but I knew God had a plan for my life. I finally had truth. Truth is a powerful thing.

We moved to Traverse City, Michigan. I thought I was ready for anything. We attended a church in town, and I was ready to serve and jumped in with both feet. I was still on the outside though because there were walls so high emotionally with me. I knew in theory I had truth, but truth by itself without the grace of God can be brutal. Because of the cover-ups in my family life and childhood, and things being swept under the rug, I had no grace. The bar was set super high. I had set a high standard for others and also myself. Well this was just a good ole set-up from the enemy. So I was in ministry and bleeding, and I didn't even know it. So of course new wounds came, and old wounds resurfaced. All someone had to do was brush up against my wounds, and it was painful. All of this was because I had no idea who I was and who God was to me. I had no real idea of what it meant to be in Christ.

If I were to be totally honest, this is something I still have to remind myself every day of my life. The old still wants to creep in. I have to renew my mind every day. I went for years being able to function in the church setting, and I knew the language. I even taught women's ministry and children's ministry about their identity in Christ. It did not penetrate my heart and soul completely. Healing comes for me in layers. God began the revealing, dealing, and healing process with me. He began to peel back the layers of my heart, only to allow me to see where I was bleeding. You can only go so long bleeding internally. It will eventually spill out. I was on the outskirts of victory. Like that cow grazing the fields, I could smell freedom, but I was not free. I could lead others there. I was still covered in works. Somehow, and I do not know how, I swallowed the lie once again that "doing" would get me there. I got my *doing* and *being* all mixed up. I tried to smash them all together, and when I did, boy did the internal quickly spill out to the external. I was a hot mess. I hit rock bottom. I was ready to throw in the towel. I felt like giving up. I could not make myself go beyond the broken fence into the wide, open space God was calling me to. Of course God, in His great mercy, knew this. He came for me. I was on the outside looking in at this spacious place. I could smell freedom. It still felt beyond my grasp. It was just out of my reach.

One day, it happened. There was an incident at church that hit a little too close to home for me. It brought up things from my childhood I thought I had moved past but clearly had not. God is so faithful. He is patient. He knows just when to pull back the curtain and show us what we need to deal with and when. All of a sudden, I became very aware of the dysfunction I had been in. Very quickly, I was not okay with the way things were. It happened really sudden. To be honest, it happened through betrayal. *Merriam-Webster* defines betrayal as the twist in the plot. You are going along just fine and then all of a sudden *wham*! Your eyes become opened. You see the dysfunction.

This happened almost overnight for me. It was like I woke up one day and said, "Wait a minute, there is something really wrong with what is happening." I began to go from this easygoing, go-with-the-flow person in ministry and life to having a real issue with what I saw happening. It didn't line up with God's Word, and my peace was gone. The mantle I carried for the ministries I was involved in was gone. I felt the full weight of the load I was carrying. God was done with me in the church I was in. I was devastated because I truly loved my pastors, friends, and the kids I taught. What I did not see is God's hand in all of it. He was calling me out to a place of freedom in Him. I was too comfortable where I was. The hard part was the betrayal. I felt betrayed, and I felt like I was also betraying the people I loved. I am loyal. I carried that burden and condemnation. So I was definitely on the outskirts of freedom but still not free.

My husband and I thought we were just tired. We were. Trying to earn righteousness is exhausting. So at first, we decided to just take a rest. We spoke to our pastors about this, and they agreed with us. We tried just coming to church and going home. This did nothing for us, yet it did wonders because when your life is not filled with the business of ministry and other things, you are able to see clearly. Once we let go of some things, we began to notice that outside of what we were doing, we had nothing left. The well was dry. We decided and talked at length with our kids about visiting other churches just for reprieve, going somewhere where no one knew us and we could just receive and go home. We wanted to get filled back up. We were depleted. We visited a church way across town. We thought no one we know would be there. We did this for a few weeks. We fell in love with the church, and we are still there today. We are home. Funny thing: feels like home is the logo our church uses. We love it. More than a new church body and building, God was calling us to a new place in Him.

The pastor of the church we are at now could sense we needed to heal, and I will never forget the very first prayer he prayed over my husband and me. It was prophetic, and I don't even know if he knows this today. We were walking out the door to go home from service, and our pastor was standing by the door as always, telling everyone bye and hugging everyone on their way out. He looked at us and saw we were really struggling. He reached out his hand and said a prayer over us, using a Bible verse. Psalm 18:19: "He brought me out into a spacious place; he rescued me because he delighted in me." Okay, coincidence? I don't think so. God was speaking. Peace came over us—the peace we had been missing—and we knew it wasn't about a cover-up or tiredness. It was God. We felt the call, and we answered.

It was still slow-going for a while. I was still carrying the load of thinking I had missed God. I missed the familiar. I wanted to drown myself in doing because it had become my safety net. I missed the ministry things. God began to woo me. That is the only words I have to describe my relationship with Him now: it is a courtship. There is a level of intimacy with God now I would have never had if the bottom had not have fallen out of my life. So there we were in a new place. It was a place of grace. We loved it. I don't know when it happened, but it happened. I quit wandering, and I started walking with purpose. God began to speak to me about personal things like my calling. I was finally out of the gate and starting to put one foot in front of the other. I had some baggage for sure so I was not moving very quickly, but I was moving. I started coming to a ladies gathering, and I met a wonderful woman who is now my spiritual mentor. The night I met her for the first time, she was speaking at the ladies gathering. It was like God Himself was speaking through her. I believe He was. She was teaching on Judas. She made a profound statement. She said this: "The only difference in the betrayal that happened with Judas and Jesus and the betrayal that happened with Peter and Jesus is that Peter accepted the gift of forgiveness and Judas did not."

This hit me so hard because the very thing that kept me back was the betrayal I felt happened. It was like God was extending His hand to me just like He did Judas right before Judas betrayed Him. There are verses in the Bible where Jesus calls him friend even though He knew what Judas was about to do to Him. It was an invitation for Judas. Right then, he could have changed his story and his role in the crucifixion of Christ. Peter did. He accepted the invitation extended to him. I began to care less about the betrayal and more about receiving God's grace for everything. This was life changing for me. I knew God was again speaking to me. It doesn't matter what happens to us or through us as much as it matters that we get God's grace on our lives. Get forgiveness. Give forgiveness. Release people. We are not to hold anyone accountable for anything. Justice is God's and God's alone.

This caused me to examine every wound through a new set of lens. When you understand we are to love as God loves and leave the rest to Him, every judgment you have made about someone else and every judgment you have made about yourself falls away. You begin to see people as God sees them. This is really freeing! Now I was ready to see all God had in store for me. I could not receive where I was before. I wasn't ready. I needed the love of my Father first. The love of the Father is critical. I will say for girls especially because we hunger and crave attention from a higher authority than ourselves. In most women, there is a longing to be protected and covered by someone bigger and stronger than them. This is by no means a sexist remark. Everyone longs to feel safe. I was beginning to feel a safety I had never experienced my whole life—the safety and love of my heavenly Father.

CHAPTER 4

THE LOVE OF MY FATHER

ONE DAY, SHE WRITES a cute little love note to a boy she met. "Dear Scotty, I love you. Do you love me? Check yes ___ or no ___." She goes out into the yard to wait for him to pass by on his bike, and her dad sees the note and asks to read it. She shows it to him with much reluctance. He then rips the note up and shames her. He tells her she is never to do that again. Girls must never write to boys. They must wait to be asked. She remembers this. It was a place of vulnerability shot down by the person she really craved love from. So she quits pursuing love and the protection from another for fear of doing the wrong thing. Never would she ever show her true feelings first.

*****

As you can imagine from my story so far, a father's love is not something I had. Oh, don't get me wrong: if you ask my earthly father if he loves me, he will say he loves me with all his heart. However, loving someone and being able to show that love when you are broken is almost impossible. Love is a verb. So I had some father issues for sure.

Growing up a pastor's daughter, and in such false doctrine and brokenness, caused me to really have an unhealthy relationship with my earthly father, which then transferred right over into my heavenly Father. Locked away emotionally in a tower is an understatement. I was emotionally shut down. So when reading the Word of God, I read from an unhealthy perspective. I did not know the author of the book. I had not really accepted His love and grace for me, so I was religious and empty. I knew how to be a good girl. On the inside, I was a mess. So I was looking out at the land and I saw a way of escape, but I also knew there were risks I had to take. In order to be really free, I had to learn to accept the love and grace of God, which means I had to be vulnerable before Him. Without the help of the Holy Spirit, this would never have happened. Being vulnerable is scary. So my hero, my knight in shining armor, began to scale the tower walls around my heart. He wooed me. He pursued me. My perspective changed. The pain of life and what happened to me began to fade. Slowly but surely, I began to get a glimpse of my heavenly Father. The pain of my past was still there, but it was in the background. This was the beginning of something beautiful.

Here is what I am learning about God, my hero, my Father in heaven:

- He is a good daddy. He thinks about me.

  O LORD, you have searched me and you know me. You know when I sit and when I rise; you perceive my thoughts from afar. You discern my going out and my lying down; you are familiar with all my ways. Before a word is on my tongue you know it completely, O LORD. I am on his mind. YOU are on his mind. (Pss. 139:1–4)

- He loves me with a perfect love. Nothing can separate me from Him and his love.

  For I am convinced that neither death nor life, neither angels nor demons, neither the present nor the future, nor any powers, neither height nor depth, nor anything else in all creation, will be able to separate us from the love of God that is in Christ Jesus our Lord. His love for me is so strong that NOTHING can separate it. (Rom. 8:37–39)

But God showed his love for us in that while we were yet sinners, Christ died for us. (Rom. 5:8)

He loves me! He loves us. His love is not with conditions. He doesn't get distracted or lose faith in us. He loves us with all our flaws, insecurities, and sin.

- He covers me. The whole Psalm chapter 103 is about the "bennies" of our Father—the benefit package, our insurance policy.

Praise the LORD, O my soul and forget not all his benefits—Who forgives all your sins and heals all your diseases, who redeems your life from the pit and crowns you with love and compassion, who satisfies your desires with good things so that your youth is renewed like the eagle's. (Pss. 103:2–5)

So in Christ, and because of the love of my Father, I have an insurance policy. I am covered.

I could go on and on with verses from the Bible about God and how our heavenly Father feels about us. There are too many to list. The Bible is God's love letter to us. When my eyes became opened to this, I began to get to know God. My relationship with Him changed and then I started to know how to take Him. Then the fun stuff starts! Because once you know how to take God, you can take Him at His word. It is a trust thing. I am not saying I have this mastered because we all have things that scare us and things we have to totally rely on God for. So we are constantly learning to trust Him.

When you know He loves you unconditionally and He has a great plan for your life, your faith increases. You can trust and have faith. Believe in the system He has in place. It is a good one. This is not easy, but it is vital. Trust is the foundation of every relationship. We have to realize God has our back, even when things aren't going our way. The interesting thing about my story is even with all the weirdness and dysfunction I grew up in, I always felt God near. He has always been there. He has been faithful.

Even though I grew up in church and had somewhat of a faith in God, my walk with Christ did not really begin until I truly came to a place of vulnerability and real true relationship with Him. I began to learn some things too. He not only began to show me who He is—God my hero, my knight in shining armor who brought me out of the tower and into the land—but also the inheritance that is mine in Christ. Intimacy with Christ is going to require giving up your running shoes. I would say I am a runner. Learning to run toward God and not away from God is where freedom is found.

CHAPTER 5

✦

IT'S ALL ABOUT THE LAND

ONE DAY, SHE, HER sister, and some friends decide they are going to steal from a candy store. Of course this was not a good decision on their part. Of course they got caught! Her mother tells her unless she pays back the money to the candy store, she will never make the highest place in heaven, for she was taught there were levels in heaven according to your good works. Where will she go? It makes her feel the heavenly realms are not enough! Is there anything better than heaven where Jesus will be there at the right hand of the Father? Is there a bad side of heaven? Ghetto heaven? This causes much confusion over where she will go and how hard she will have to work to earn that high place. It was then and there she becomes focused on herself and getting good enough instead of the hero who died so she could one day be with Him forever.

*****

I am a landowner. You are a landowner. In the biblical days, if you were a landowner, you were considered wealthy. This is symbolic for those who are in Christ. Inheriting the land is a theme throughout Scripture, and it is a message to us as believers. It started in Genesis. The first thing God did after the creation of man was to give him the guided tour and layout of the land in the garden and all that was available to Adam and Eve. It is symbolic to us as His creation.

Everything that belongs to God belongs to us. We are heirs to the throne in Christ.

Ephesians 1:13 says, "And you also were included in Christ when you heard the word of truth, the gospel of your salvation. Having believed, you were marked in him with a seal, the promised Holy Spirit, who is a deposit guaranteeing our inheritance until the redemption of those who are God's possession—to the praise of his glory." So we are promised an inheritance in Christ. As God's chosen ones, He set it all up for us. We have an inheritance in Him. So every time you read about a promise from God to man in the Bible, most of the time, there will be mention of land. In Exodus, in Joshua, in Deuteronomy, but especially in Genesis when God made a promise to Abraham, there is a promise to bring Abraham to the land God wanted him to have for him and his descendants. That is you and I. We are landowners. We are descendants of Abraham.

> The LORD had said to Abram, "Leave your country your people and your father's household and go to the land I will show you.
> "I will make you into a great nation and I will bless you;
> "I will make your name great, and you will be a blessing. I will bless those who bless you, and whoever curses you I will curse; and all the peoples on the earth will be blessed through you." (Gen. 12:1–3)

So we are seeds of Abraham. We are in Christ. The blessings of Abraham are ours. When God makes mention of the land, it is a representation of our inheritance. He wants us to know what He has for us as His children, and He wants us to take Him at His word.

> If you belong to Christ, then you are Abraham's seed, and heirs according to the promise. (Gal. 3:29)

Heirs to what? The land! It is all about the land. Taking up our inheritance is like cashing in the golden ticket. We have to know who we are and whose we are. Who do you belong to?

Once I started to get ahold of this and realized I have a place at the table with Christ right now, the feelings of shame, guilt, and condemnation had no place in my life. Knowing He has clothed me in His righteousness, when He looks at me, God looks at me through eyes of grace and redemption. He sees the finished work of the cross when He looks at me. This is the best balm I have ever received for any wound I received. I had to accept the gift.

> And God raised us up with Christ and seated us with him in the heavenly realms in Christ Jesus, in order that in the coming ages he might show the incomparable riches of his grace, expressed in his kindness to us in Christ Jesus. For it is by grace you have been saved, through faith-and this not from yourselves, it is the gift of God—not by works, so that no man can boast. (Eph. 2:6–9)

Salvation and the grace of God are gifts. We can't earn it. We do not qualify so stop trying to get good enough and accept the gift. This is what needed to happen with me. You see, I believed in Jesus, but I was not living out my full salvation. I was still trying to earn my way in. I didn't really know the carpenter. He was the one who was there guiding me and shaping me through every situation. One of the things that helped me break out of the tower was finding my place in Christ. My mother helped with this, and she doesn't even realize it. Her church believes there are levels to heaven based on your spiritual growth (don't ask). I was always looking at my mistakes and thinking I would never make it to the top—the highest place in the heavenly realms. Maybe just heaven. Maybe I will make heaven. The church I was raised in believes there is a higher place than heaven where only the overcomers will go. This is the people who are able to live a separated life totally different than the world. They are the ones who can grow their hair out and not cuss, spit, or chew—you know the ones.

One day, my mother was trying to tell me in the only way she knew how God had given her peace about my walk with Him. She said, "I am not sure where in heaven you are going, but I know you are going."

Again, I asked, "Is there a slummy part of heaven?" Somehow I doubt that! My God doesn't cut corners, value one life over another, or show partiality.

At that moment, something rose up in me, and I became angry. I don't ever disrespect my parents, but something came over me. I finally told my mother exactly where I am going. The Bible says I have heavenly seating with Christ right now. I am in Christ, and I am with Christ right now according to Ephesians chapter 2. I began to take ahold of what is mine in Christ Jesus. You see, it is not enough to see the land. It is not enough to walk around the edges of it hoping one day the giants will go away and you will conquer it. I had to decide I was willing to fight for it. I had to face the giants in the land, and I had to take my place. I had to know what is mine.

In order to go in the land, you need some identification. You must have your passport out. Know who you are. Proof of your identity is vital. If I had a wealthy relative and they passed away and left an inheritance to me, I would have to show up at the reading of the will with proof of who I am in tow. In order to claim it, I would have to show my identity to the person in authority. It is no different with our inheritance in Christ. Believe me, the villain knows exactly who you are.

He is constantly trying to take away your inheritance. He tries to steal your identity too.

So what is ours?

- Adoption into the family of God (Eph. 1:3–6)
- Freedom from condemnation (Rom. 8:1–4)
- Friendship in Christ (John 15:15)
- Blessed with every spiritual blessing (Rom. 8:32, 1 Cor. 3:21–23)

- Unconditional love of the Father (John 15:9, 16:27)
- No longer under the law (Gal. 2:19–21)
- Joint heirs with Christ (Rom. 8:17)

And the list goes on and on! For me, when I started really seeing the land, the inheritance given to me, that is when I started to really experience joy and peace, and my faith became stronger. So it is all about the land. When this happens, you want to share it with others who need it. I wanted to shout it from the rooftops when I learned about my inheritance in Christ. I practice this daily. I am the righteousness of Christ. I am chosen. I was chosen before the foundation of the world destined to rule and reign with Christ. I am seated with Christ right now in heavenly places. I have heavenly seating. A royal seat at the table is arranged for me daily. It is my place. Like little Fibby at King David's table, I have a place! No one can take my place. God finds me irreplaceable and irresistible; I am his.

These words have to be on the front of our passport. They have to be visible for the enemy to see. He needs to see you are thinking of your place all the time. It is always on your mind. Believe me, it is on the enemy's mind. He left all of that and has much regret. He does not want us to take our rightful place. He would rather us hide out in our wounds and in fear. He certainly does not want us to help others get there.

So how do we "take the land"? I am free in Christ, but like so many others with passports in their pockets, it is easy to put yourself back in unhealthy places. Remember you didn't get dysfunctional overnight. So freedom takes time and work on your part. I use the word *work* with some fear and a little bit cautiously. Let me say this: you are going to have to stay free on purpose. This comes with time, retraining yourself on how to respond to the enemy when he comes after you. I will share with you what has helped me.

We are in the land and it is ours and we are free. We have proper ID. Do we know how to walk that out? What does that look like? For me, I have had the theory of this but not enough experience. This takes time. We need to get familiar with all we have access to. We can't walk it alone. We need the hero there doing His work in us, causing us to grow and transform. In order for this to happen, we are going to experience times when we need to use what God has given us. He has given us tools. This means we are going to have to use them. We are going to go through some things that are going to cause us to reach out and take hold of what is ours.

Practical application is the only thing that works. We can know in theory what we have, but that was my biggest problem. I knew in my head I was God's child, but until it becomes an experience, it is just a lot of knowledge. Good information, and that is all. The wonderful hero will be there for every step you take through your land. When my daughter was little, she and my husband loved to go on hikes through the woods. They called it "going on a bear hunt." They would pack a lunch and go on these adventures. They loved it. We get to do this same thing with our hero, Jesus. At times, we get into scrapes and scratches and maybe encounter a wild animal or two, but the hero of our story is there to rescue us every time.

Part of doing the work is allowing the Holy Spirit to deal with our hearts when we fear and have thoughts that do not line up with how God sees us. We live in a fleshly body, and we have to really pay attention to our heart and take care of it. I will be going along and thinking things are fine and then an old thought of unworthiness or condemnation will come up, and it takes me back to a place of slavery and bondage. There are some things I am learning that are helping me. We are going to fail sometimes. When we do, it is easy to beat ourselves up and feel defeated, but this is a good thing when we fail. It is an opportunity to lean on Jesus and his grace and forgiveness. The enemy will also always try to make you agree with his assessment of your situation. He wants you to believe a lie. So when you mess up and you are feeling weak, this is when the enemy comes after you. When we are weak and vulnerable, he attacks. Most of the time, we don't even see it coming.

In order to receive all God has for us, we have to let go of what we are holding on to. I ask you: what is in your hands right now? What thoughts plague your mind at night while you try to sleep? What relationship are you in that does not nourish your soul or bring you closer to freedom? I know, I know, I am asking a ton of questions here, but the things we love the most sometimes are the things that bring us the most pain. Everyone has a past and relationships they have had to leave behind either by their choice or by something beyond their control. It is painful. This is going to sound generic, but it is worth sharing. Every time I lose something, or God requires me to let go of something, He always replaces *and...* it is always better! Maybe not at the time because, let's face it, a breakup is a breakup, and there is pain associated with it. We have to learn how to travel lighter. Not everything we are carrying is ours. If it feels too heavy, it is. Jesus says, "My burdens are easy and my yoke is light." This is not to suggest we will need to let go of every hard thing but of the things that maybe aren't helpful to us in where we are going next.

Some people are not going to choose freedom. Not only will they refuse it but, they will slow you down and cause your heart much harm in the process. When we choose to walk with God in the land, there will be times that we will walk it alone. Not really alone, but there will be times it will just be you and God, your wonderful hero, your knight in shining armor, walking some things out. Even family members and people you can't imagine living life without will be distant for you at times, especially if they are not going to choose true freedom in Christ.

The saying "You can't get to Canaan hanging on to Egypt" is so true. This was a quote from a pastor friend of mine. It is such a true statement. Once you have a made up your mind that you are going to take hold of everything that is yours and be a landowner, then your focus has to be on the land you are in. So there are things from the past that are going to creep up from time to time. The key is recognizing them for what they are. Some things are just not meant to be. What I am going to share next is tough, but it is key to healing and peace. There are people who may have once played an important role in your life but may not make it to your land with you. Even family. This is hard, but even in the body of Christ, I have experienced loss because I will be doing life with people I love and it will one day just become obvious we are not going in the same direction at all. You love people always, but recognizing that even a person can be Egypt and represent the past for you for you is hard.

I have had to let go of people I loved with all my heart, and because our paths no longer crossed and God's direction for me and His direction for them was different, we no longer see each other. Other times, there have just been unhealthy bonds God did not want for me, and I have had to let people go. You can do this lovingly, and you should, but let's face it: a breakup is still a breakup. It hurts! So there is no going back! You have to move forward in your land knowing God will provide for you all that you need. He will take care of your past, present, and future relationships. Move on.

There are places you may have once felt comfortable going that you will no longer visit. It happens. Once your spirit becomes aware of what you have in Christ, some places will just not satisfy you.

There will also be places that remind you of the past, and it is just good not to go back. That is Egypt for you. If it takes you back to an unhealthy thought or memory, get out. You do not belong there. Some of us need to tear the rearview mirrors off our cars and drive away. No looking back. The only reason to ever look back is to help someone else get out if they want out.

I have done some house cleaning. Spiritually speaking, we get a clean house when we decide we are going to take ownership of the land. Physically, we may need to clean our house out. I did. There were books, pictures, and mementos that took me to an unhealthy place, and one day, I packed it all up and put it in the trashcan. If it needed to be donated, I donated it. It's not that there was anything wrong per se with the things I was holding on to; it was more that they were a reminder of Egypt for me. They symbolized something that no longer held meaning in my life. The stuff had to go. We need to do this mentally as well. There are thoughts that creep in and want to take up residence in your life; get rid of them!

We recently built a house, and the house we sold was one we had lived in for nine years. Wow, did we ever have stuff to clean out! This is the same for us spiritually speaking. We accumulate a lot of junk, and sometimes we need to do a clean-up. It is amazing to me the amount of things we carry that are not ours. We are like sponges sometimes, and we have to be intentional about making sure we are emptying out in a healthy way. This is especially true if you work with people. We tend to take things on that are not meant for us to carry. This can be people. We can carry people. We can carry stuff like it is our very own. I would say 99.99999 percent of things that weigh heavily on our minds are things we have no control over. We need to let go. Travel light! You will have the energy to go farther and be more effective for the kingdom. It is all God's business.

> The child grew and was weaned, and on the day Isaac was weaned Abraham held a great feast. But Sarah saw that the son whom Hagar the Egyptian had borne to Abraham was mocking, and she said to Abraham, "Get rid of that slave woman and her son, for that slave woman and her son will never share in the inheritance with my son Isaac." (Gen. 21:8–10)

In Genesis 21:8–10, we read the exchange between Abraham and Sarah. Abraham had two sons. One was with a slave woman, and the other was with his wife whom he was in a covenant relationship with. Sarah, his wife, saw the son of the slave woman who, by the way, was not a part of the promise was mocking her son, Isaac, who was the promised heir, so she called for a separation. "Get rid of the slave woman and her son." This is a great picture of what I am trying to share about taking hold of our promise. Our past mistakes, relationships, and failures creep up on us. We are sometimes really tied to them in an unhealthy way. Even blood ties!

This is a hard one! I have had to walk this out. It is painful. It has held me captive for so long, and I carried the weight of someone else's sin and captivity for so long. God is setting me free from it. The only time I want it to show up in my life is for God to get glory from it. I have restoration in my heart, but reconciliation is God's to handle. I let go. My parents are elderly and in oppression, depression, addiction, and spiritual bondage. I have witnessed to them. I have supported them and loved them, and now I have let them go. God's promise for me is for them too. He loves us all, but we are going in completely different directions. The fleshly unhealthy ties have been cut. They are in the hands of the hero of the story. Jesus will come for them like He has me. My prayer is that they climb over the walls and into His loving arms this side of eternity.

Just like the slave woman in Genesis and the free, separation has to come. Otherwise, in the words of my pastor when he taught the message of Genesis chapter 21, "your mistake will mock your miracle." What God has set you free from will still be right there to mock you unless you put some distance between it and you. If you are walking toward freedom and there is a relationship in your life that is harmful, maybe it's time. Let it go. Empty your hands of the fleshly so God can fill your hands with the promise. Obviously, I am not referring to covenant relationships such as marriage or healthy family squabbles. I am talking destructive thought patterns, places, or relationships that harm. This is tough stuff, but it has been my journey to freedom and God is near.

It is time to let go. How do you let go the right way?

CHAPTER 6

LIES AND AGREEMENTS

WHAT WILL SHE BECOME? Is she just a wife and mother? Does she have a story to tell? Should she just try to blend in? Going with the flow seems safe even in her newfound freedom. Yet the desire is there; the longing to discover what God has graced her to do. Can she? Will she? There it is—that tug on her heartstrings. It is like holding the string of what she thinks is a kite, but she isn't sure what is on the other end. It is pulling her, and she feels compelled to go.

*****

A huge part of letting go is finding the freedom to be you. When this happens, there is always a natural breakaway that happens in relationships because sometimes people like you when they think you are going to be what they want you to be. But when your true self, with all the unique gifting and callings, start to rise up, some people will not embrace the new you or, should I say, the true you. God has gifted each one of us with special gifts only we have. Part of the journey to my freedom is when I truly seek to please God and embrace what He has gifted me with. When I begin to love myself and really walk in the specific call God has, I am free. We must get into agreement with God about what those things are.

It's very easy to look at someone who is successful and think, "It's easy for them, but I will never get there." It's easy to see the gifts that God has graced another person and wish He had given that to you. You see, what God has graced you with can sometimes be hard to embrace because we feel the work, labor-intensive effort, and devotion that will have to come to make it happen. Writing this book is something I feel God has graced me to do. It's hard! It has not been easy. One of the ways we get there is by embracing the gifts God has given us. Until we come into agreement with God on what He has given us, we will never fully walk out the life of fulfillment and freedom we are meant to have. This is going to take some discipline. It is going to take some discipline of the mind. Let me ask you this question: who are you agreeing with about your future?

Jesus, the hero of your story, has a plan for your life. Satan, the villain in our story, also has a plan for your life. Who are you agreeing with?

> Let this mind be in you, which was also in Christ Jesus. (Phil. 2:7)

> For, "Who has known the mind of the Lord so as to instruct him?" But we have the mind of Christ. (1 Cor. 2:16)

So there is a daily maintenance we need to do to function at the level God wants us to function at. We must renew our mind. I am finding this is not a one-time, per-day thing. This is constant. The thoughts that hit our mind are coming in at record speed sometimes.

My victory comes when I go to Jesus first and ask Him to help me in my walk and in all that my day holds and then ask God to cover my mind with His love. It sometimes goes like this:

> Lord Jesus, I come to you today and I ask that you give me your thoughts and your love for this day. Cover my mind and my heart so I may think like you think and love as you love. Any thoughts I may have that are contrary to your word and your thoughts about me, I cast them off

today. Help me get on board with your thoughts about me and your love for me and your love for other people. Help me love as you love. Father, I come into agreement with you about my life and your plans for it. I cooperate with you in this. I am fully on board with you.

This is a start. Then throughout your day, as you are working and doing what the day requires, should you start to feel weighed down by the day and the circumstances, go back to that prayer. Begin to thank God that by faith you asked for His mind, and by faith you believe you received it. Renew, recalibrate, and regroup. This is an everyday thing for me. We have to pay attention to what we are thinking and whom we are agreeing with. For me, this is so important. It is important for my emotional health and especially my spiritual health.

I can't say enough about healthy mindset. Perspective is everything! I have come to realize the enemy never stops shooting his fiery darts at us, and he does it by overwhelming our minds with thoughts that are negative. He wants us to make an agreement with him about them.

I have heard the saying that where the mind goes, the man will follow. This is so true. So it is a constant battle we are in to have healthy thoughts about our heavenly Father, ourselves, and others.

One of the biggest things we have to know in order to have victory is we are in a war zone. We live in a fallen world, so keeping an uncluttered mind is key. One of the strategies in war is distraction. This all starts in the mind and keeps us from walking out the call of God on our lives. It also just keeps us from enjoying life.

It is easier sometimes to just go along our merry way and not see the battle we are in because, let's face it, at times, it can be exhausting trying to keep a disciplined mind. So I think I have to spend some time to share what I am learning about the strategy of the enemy and how the villain comes after me. In doing so, I am sure you will be able to relate since he pretty much does the same to all who are in Christ.

Distraction is huge in warfare against the enemy. This book is not a book on warfare, but it has to be mentioned because if we don't get a good understanding of our lives and the environment in which we have been planted in, we won't ever see it coming. We need to know the players in our story—all of them. Being unaware is being unprepared. This puts us at such a disadvantage with the enemy.

So the first tactic I experience with the enemy is distraction. If the enemy can keep you in a negative thought process about God, yourself, or the people in your life, he has you beat. He uses humanity as his advantage. Some people give him great material to work with. He uses our imperfections as a distraction to us. It is really hard to have a good attitude when someone else's flaws distract you. We are all flawed. He uses this to grab our attention and get the focus off Jesus, our hero and our Savior, and on to the person. He then causes conflict. It all starts with distraction.

This is what causes people to be offended and leave churches or not even attend at all. Most of the time, when distraction comes, I don't even recognize it for what it is. I automatically get involved and then when the conflict comes, I finally realize I once again took my eyes off Jesus and put it on the situations going on around me. That causes me to feel defeated.

Fighting against distraction is key in having a sound mind. We must make up our minds that while we are not perfect at detecting when something is going to be a distraction, we can be intentional about keeping the mind of Christ in every situation. I was researching distractions, and I read a quote from *The Art of War* by Sun Tzu.

The strategy to win without fighting: a situation where one side wins by putting the other side at such a massive disadvantage that the issue of fighting it out never comes up. They quit before the war ever starts because they are exhausted by the thought of what might happen! The disadvantage to the enemy that will cause him to disengage is when he can't find any chinks in the armor because we are so focused on the hero of the story, Jesus Christ. Our focus is completely on Christ. This is the key to complete victory. Fighting the battle in victory, not for victory.

It is the only way to win without going into complete knock-down, drag-out warfare. He also distracts by trying to get us to carry on a dialog with him. Do not address the enemy. Address your thoughts and invite the Lord of lords and King of kings to come right in the middle of the dialog the enemy is trying to have with you mentally.

Have you ever had a thought and wondered, "Where in the world did that come from?" Chances are, if it was random and unlike something you would think about or say, it wasn't you. Yeah, that's right. I am saying you are hearing voices. Sounds weird. The Bible talks about the fiery darts of the enemy. So he does this by shooting thoughts at our mind and causing us to derail because it's usually so off the wall or feels like truth that, before we know it, we have agreed with the enemy that it is truth. This keeps people in bondage. We must understand not every thought we have is our own. It is coming straight from the pit of hell, and we need to send it to the cross and not make agreements with our enemy about ourselves or our family members or what could happen or anything else that does not line up with God and His word. Even if something is happening and it looks bad, invite Jesus in right away.

His thoughts are higher than our thoughts
and his ways are higher than our ways. (Isa. 55:9)

This is tough because until we make a choice to be intentional about this, we will not even notice war is being waged against us.

Think what God thinks about *you*.

For every awful situation that happened to me as a child and even into adulthood, there was an ugly message from the evil one that was sent to me. It is not an easy thing to do, but if you are struggling with your past and it keeps creeping up or you just feel stuck and you don't even know why, ask God to show you where you have made agreements with the villain in your life and in your story.

I don't wallow in my past, but the truth is there is profit in going back and breaking every agreement that was made and allowing God to erase the messages written on your heart by the evil one and replace them with God's truth. Let me explain what an agreement looks like and how to break it. The easiest way to break an agreement with your enemy is to agree with what God says about you in His word.

When my dad innocently shamed me for writing the love note, as I shared in an earlier chapter, right then, the enemy was there. The lie that was whispered to me was showing vulnerability was wrong, and it caused me to hold a piece of myself back. That stuck with me, and I didn't even realize it. So years later, when I was doing a study on intimacy with God, He was faithful to remind me of that memory. I began to pray and agree with what God's Word says about coming to Him with any and everything that was on my heart.

> So let us come boldly to the throne of our gracious God. (Heb. 4:16, NLT)

Another word for *bold* is the word *blunt*. To be blunt, you must be open, honest, and vulnerable. So my prayer life became more open, honest, and raw. Once I understood that I don't have to hide what I am really feeling from God, the level of intimacy I gained with God was amazing. I can tell Him anything! He is not shocked, disappointed, or angry. After venting to God about all that is bothering you and casting your cares on Him, it is important to agree with God on the matter. I struggle with this, but it is vital. At the end of the day, when all the crying is over and the emotions of whatever it is you are struggling with are quieted, God's Word is still true. He is still God and He is on the throne and He will take care of you and yours.

Confession is also the key. The enemy needs to hear you say it. God's got this! I will trust you God even though I can't see the way out. Agree with God about relationships. Agree with Him about the broken ones. I once posted on social media about breaking ties with unhealthy people and how sometimes it is even needed in family situations. I don't believe God wants that, but there are times when it is unhealthy to stay in situations that will do you harm. So many people responded to the post because brokenness in families is so real and raw. It is hurtful. Begin to agree with what God says about your loved ones.

Ask God to come for them as He does us when we are lost. One of my favorite sayings is "*love beyond words.*" It is a little sign I have siting on my desk in my office. It is a reminder that sometimes you have said all the words you can say. *We* need to be done talking and posting. Instead, the best way to love someone who has hurt or continues to hurt you with their choices and their own brokenness is to bless them. This is in agreement with God. God's heart for all of us is to bless us.

> Blessed is he who comes in the name of the
> LORD. From the house of the LORD we bless
> you. (Ps. 118:26, NIV)

We—God and I—I come into agreement with God.

Who do you need to bless right now? Who has been the center of your thoughts for way too long? Take a moment right now. It's okay. Bless them. Speak words of life over them. If it never affects them, I promise you, it will affect you. Your heart longs to be free. Every time the nagging thoughts come back, say a blessing over them. This gets the attention of our hero. He loves it! He is near.

So learning about lies and agreements from the evil one has been huge in my journey toward wholeness. I have a feeling it will be in yours too. I pray that as you are reading this, you will begin to feel hope. We can get through anything with the help of Jesus. He knows just when to swoop in and carry us. He knows when we need to walk it out and stand firm in faith. I say it a lot in this story because it is true. He is near.

CHAPTER 7

✦

SHAME

STANDING IN GYM CLASS. All the other children are dressed in their gym clothing. She is still wearing the shirt and full skirt her mother sent her to school in. The gym teacher is frustrated with her because today is aerobics. This includes flips and cartwheels and whatever else the teacher wants to do to get these children active and moving. She stands in fear along the wall, hoping since she does not have the proper clothing to participate, maybe she will get a pass. She is trying to be invisible. No such luck. She is given a pair of boy's swimming trunks—bright red and Speedo-style—and instructed to wear them under her skirt. Her underpants were still showing, which became the topic of discussion with the other students. Shame you think? She wanted to just disappear.

*****

I am very familiar with shame. It has been my constant companion since I was old enough to recognize I was different than other kids. I was dressed differently. I stood out like a sore thumb. This was back in the late seventies and early eighties. You really just want to blend in.

Because of the strict doctrine of the church my family attended, I stood out like a zebra in a herd of elephants, so there is that type of shame and embarrassment I was very familiar with and then there is the shame that comes from feelings of inadequacy or feeling like you will never measure up. It's too late for you, or because of your story, you are permanently flawed. There is something fundamentally wrong that causes you to not be able to function on the level that others do. This is a victim mentality that is brought on by shame. We have to talk about shame because it is vital to freedom. I have seen God go to great lengths to pursue the heart of people I love, and because they are so covered in shame, they can't recognize it. It is like sitting in a jail cell with the doors wide open and not being able to walk out because they are cloaked in shame.

This was me as well. Until I faced the shame of my story, I couldn't really walk out. I was sitting in a class for wounds held at my church, and there was a group of eight people sitting in a close circle. This was a confidential group. It was a safe place created by the leaders of the class to allow people to share their story with the others in the group. I will never forget this. It is getting close to the end of the evening, and it was my turn to share my story with the group. I remember fumbling my way through bits and pieces of my story and then it was time to go home. There wasn't even really time for people to react to all I had shared. I went home and just felt so ashamed. I remember feeling that way, and one thing I learned from being in that healing class was to investigate. If you can't shake a bad feeling or thought and it is plaguing you, there is a lie attached to it. The villain is there trying to get you to see your situation from his viewpoint. He is all wrapped up in your business. He is trespassing.

So through prayer and God's spirit, I began to recognize shame was what I was feeling and I could get rid of it and be free from it. Half of the battle is knowing what you are dealing with. So once I began to recognize and identify shame, I could put the truth of God's Word to it. What does the Word of God say about shame?

For me, being a rule follower was important, and out of that came much brokenness and shame. Trying to be a good girl with bad information—this is my story. I had a high standard for myself and for everyone else too, so the shame that followed my story was horrific. It was failure. I could not succeed with the standards set before me. The truth is no one could! Christ came not to abolish the law according to Matthew but to fulfill it. No one can live up to the law especially manmade law.

We need God's grace and mercy for our regrets and our shame.

The first place where we see shame in the Bible is Genesis. Adam and Eve sinned, and all of a sudden, they are fully aware of their nakedness. It caused them to feel shame, and they went into hiding. What I find most interesting about this story is this is also the first time atonement is made for sin and covenant with God is introduced. They made their own covering out of fig leaves, which is exactly what we try to do when we sin. We find a quick cover-up. God comes calling in the cool of the day, and He uncovers their sin. Something has to die in order to cover it, so He makes them a covering from animal skins. This is a shadow and type of the new covenant He would make with all of mankind for the atonement of sin. Something had to die, and that was Jesus Christ, His Son. This took care of every past, present, or future sin. It abolished the law and brought life to all who would receive.

> "Do not think I have come to abolish the Law or the Prophets; I have not come to abolish them but to fulfill them." (Matt. 5:17, NIV)

This is important. So we could not ever measure up! This is why God sent His son to die on the cross. He came to fulfill and be the ultimate sacrifice and to atone for all we have ever done or will ever do.

Furthermore, the Bible has specific things to say about shame.

> Having canceled the written code, with its regulations, that was against us and that stood opposed to us; he took it away, nailing it to the cross. And having disarmed the powers and authorities, he made a public spectacle of them, triumphing over them by the cross. (Col. 2:14–15, NIV)

Our sin is nailed to the cross forevermore.

So to God be the glory! All the things that plague you and embarrass you have been nailed to the cross. Every accusation truly or falsely written against you or spoken over you has been nailed to the cross. Jesus took away our shame. Can we forget it too? Can we recognize that the enemy has no power except the power we give him? I hope so!

In order to really be free, I had to see shame for what it is. It is old stuff. It was yesterday's stuff. It doesn't belong in today. Jesus took out the trash. Don't allow the enemy to talk you into dumpster diving! You have been redeemed!

If you are in Christ and have accepted His grace, you have made the trade.

> Instead of your shame you will receive a double portion, and instead of disgrace you will rejoice in your inheritance. And so you will inherit a double portion in your land, and everlasting joy will be yours. (Isa. 61:7, NIV)

So if you haven't made the trade yet, it is a good deal!

This is part of taking your inheritance and taking ownership of your land and your life. No shame. We know we need Jesus. We will make mistakes. I make huge ones. Jesus has me covered. I am not that little girl in third grade standing against the wall in gym class hoping I am invisible. I am a daughter of the most high God. He sees me, and I no longer have to hide out in shame. I don't have to be ashamed of my story and how I got here. I am grateful for my story now because I can share it with others, and my past wounds can bring healing. It is no longer a victim mentality but a victorious one, and God can receive all the glory in my story.

I sin. You sin. We all sin. It is one thing to recognize the feeling of conviction and guilt. Guilt means you are guilty. Being guilty and shameful are two completely different things. Guilt means you sinned and are in need of a Savior. If you recognize this, it is a good thing. Shame is different. It makes you feel like you are hopeless to change and then the hiding comes. If you mess up, confess it to God, get His forgiveness, and repent, and with the power of the Holy Spirit on your side, turn. Repentance is not just being sorrowful about your mistake; that is remorse sometimes brought on by guilt. Repentance is the desire to do better. We desire to do better not so God will accept us but *because* God has already accepted us. Out of our love for Him, we will want to live a life that brings Him glory. For me, it is not about striving for perfection but more of a pursuit of Jesus Christ Himself. Time with Him and a pursuit of Him brings about changes I can never make on my own.

I don't speak as if I have arrived. If I have given that impression, then I have failed miserably at what I believe I am supposed to do. No way have I arrived. I am walking this out with God's help. The hero of my story wants to be the hero in yours. He pursues us with all of our flaws, and He never gives up on us.

Don't give up on you. You are worth it.

How do we recognize shame?

Here are some indicators:

1. The hesitancy to be around other people

    I know that some people are just naturally shy and prefer time to themselves versus time with others, but there is an unhealthy balance we can have when we totally go into isolation. This is a good sign you are dealing with shame in some way.

2. Defensiveness or the urge to cast blame

    Shame leads to blame. Adam and Eve did this in the garden. Adam told God it was the woman God gave him, thus blaming God and Eve. Eve said it was the serpent's fault. All was because of shame.

3.   Feelings of unworthiness or body-image issues

   This is the direct result of shame in some form or another.

4.   An inability to embrace vulnerability or show your true feelings

   Shame is at the bottom of it. A fear that expressing one's true feelings will result in some sort of humiliation or dismissal of who you are.

I could go on and on because I have found that shame rears its ugly head in all things, and we have to speak out against it. In order to do this, we have to speak in the authority of the one who nailed it to the cross once and for all. I found that with my story, shame was a thread that was woven throughout the pages in such a way that I was uncomfortable with who I was and where I came from, and for years, it has kept me from really stepping into the call God has on my life. I see it now. I deal with it when it rears its ugly head and I have to call it out for what it is. Like the great and powerful Oz behind the curtain, when you pull back the curtain, it is this puny, little, good-for-nothing accusation and lie from the enemy, and we must unmask it and render it powerless before the cross of Calvary where Jesus took it all on Himself. Since Jesus did this, we can now walk in authority as His child. No more shame. No more blame. No more running.

CHAPTER 8

ALL AUTHORITY

ONE DAY, SHE DECIDES to return to the home of her childhood. It is so much smaller than what she remembers it being as a child. She walks the ground of the castle and sees no life there. No one lives there anymore. All that was once home to her seems stale, and all the things that seemed so gigantic to her seem so small. She realizes it isn't so much that it's smaller but that she has grown. What was once a painful place to be has no power over her to make her run or cower. She anticipates the familiarity of it rather than dreading it. She is walking the grounds now with a sense of peace because she is not alone. He is near...

*****

Authority—when we truly understand this word, we will be free. I know it is a huge statement to make, but it is really true. Understanding is half the battle. To truly walk in our calling and live a life that brings God's glory into our story, we have to approach things God's way.

Walking in the authority of Jesus Christ is the only way to really truly live. Everything else is just coping. I have spent a lot of years just coping. Band-Aid salvation. Bleeding on the inside with God's Word sitting right in my lap. The church I grew up in focused mainly on the Old Testament in the Bible. The Old Testament was before the covenant between God and man was recorded, so my approach to God and His Word was old. It was filled with manmade laws and really just a twisted version of the Word of God at best. When I began to fully understand that we have authority to walk this earth as Jesus walked, doing the things Jesus did, the walls came crashing down the rest of the way. We are still under God's authority, but for most believers, we are not walking in all of it. I wasn't. I still am so shocked when I ask God and I am in faith and I am believing God for something, and He does it. Usually, He goes far above all I ask for since I put limits on Him because my mind doesn't think like His does. I ask Him to do things that I think would bring me joy, and He does things that are for the good of all that are involved, not just me.

This is who God is. This is covenant prayers being answered. Under the new covenant God has given us through His son going to the cross, we now can ask God for anything, and if it is in line with His will, it will be done. This is us lining up with God and praying with God for things that need to happen here on earth. This is vital to my story, and I will share with you the reason why: my family. They are still in bondage, and I want to come into agreement with God about their lives. My parents are in false doctrine and slaves to religion and law. God wants to set them free. My job is to align my heart to God's plan and pray and believe that this will happen. I speak no disrespect over another denomination or church affiliation except when I see that a person is going to be lost. This is biblical to pray for them that God, the beautiful hero of my story, will come for them just like He has for me.

> "I tell you the truth, whatever you bind on earth will be bound in heaven, and whatever you loose on earth will be loosed in Heaven.
>
> "Again, I tell you that if two of you on earth agree about anything you ask for, it will be done for you by my Father in heaven. For where two or three come together in my name, there I am with them." (Matt. 18:18–19)

This is Jesus speaking to His disciples. He is telling them the authority they have in prayer when they come together and agree about the things that are in the heavenly realms.

God doesn't just want to free you, but He is after all involved in our story. This is who He is. So for me to understand how to pray for the lost loved ones who need Jesus to rescue them, I have to pray like He prays. You have to pray and think of people as Jesus does. This is walking in the authority given to us by God.

If every sin was nailed to the cross and every victory is already won because of the shedding of the precious blood of Jesus, then our prayers for our lost loved ones are this:

> Jesus, in your mighty and precious name that is above every name, we come into agreement with you that every knee will bow and every tongue will confess that you are King of kings and Lord of lords. Time doesn't mean anything to you here. You are not limited to time or space, so right now in heaven, these things are happening. Let us witness these things here and now on earth. Whatever is bound in heaven, let it be bound on earth, and whatever is loosed in heaven concerning my loved ones, let it be loosed here now on earth.

This, my friends, is praying in the authority given to you as God's child.

The truth is shame, doubt, fear, and failures of the past can't stand up under this type of praying. It all melts away in the presence of the Almighty. This is what the fight is about. God wants to use us to further His kingdom. As long as we stay stuck in our own story, He can't because there is no kingdom like prayers going up when we are engrossed in the wrong done to us. It is a self-focus that keeps us stuck. If you are reading this book, then I have to tell you that God is calling you out of the trenches of your own shame and fully into His presence where your new role will be to pray for those who have affected you in your story and those you have also affected. It is a ministry of reconciliation, and God is calling you just like He is me. We must get past our past. Tear the rearview mirrors off, begin to engage in kingdom prayers, and walk in our full authority with Jesus. So authority plays a huge role in our freedom. Every morning, we must align ourselves up with God and His authority. Ask God to show you how to have His thoughts and His ways. His thoughts are higher than ours, and His ways are better. This is really doing life with Jesus every day. Don't just live for God; live life with God. Include Him on all things. Walk in your authority as His child. Take the land. This is crossing over Jordan. This is entering your promised land.

Authority is the power or right to give orders, make decisions, and enforce obedience (*Merriam-Webster's* definition)

So in order to walk in our full authority, we must come into the obedience of Christ ourselves. This is going to take some denying of ourselves to do so.

I used the word *align* earlier. I am going to have to expand on it. We are made up of three distinct parts. There is our spirit. Then we all have a soul. We also have this physical body we live in.

Our spirit becomes whole upon salvation. This is where the spirit of God dwells in us. He takes up residence in our spirit when we invite Him in. Our soul is another matter altogether. Our soul we will wrestle with until we are with Jesus in heaven. Our bodies house it all. It is the shell of who we are. Our soul is where we find our mind/conscience, our will, and our emotions. This soul has to be aligned with the heart and mind of God every day. It needs regeneration and renewing all the time.

To walk in the full authority of Jesus means we have to give up our rights to justice. It is God who justifies. It is God who saves. It is God who redeems, and God calls the shots. So for all of us who want to go back to the person/persons who harmed us and get healing there... forget that. Go to God. He is your healer. Unless God has redeemed that person/persons, they will never be able to give you what you are looking for and then the trap of the enemy unfolds. You will stay in your wounds, and kingdom prayers will never happen through you. Oh, my friends, I hope I am getting through to you. This is where I live. Every day is a choice to move forward with the mind of Christ and walk in my God-given authority or stay stuck in the muck. For me, the temptation is always there because the people who have harmed me are still out there doing that same thing to others. Here's the deal. They are God's. He is big enough to handle them. God gets all the glory when we make a choice to push past our soul and into the spirit of God within us and lift up a kingdom-minded prayer on the behalf of those who need it. Praying for those who wrong you is probably one of the most selfless things you can do. Jesus did this as He was dying: "Father, forgive them…"

I know it isn't going to be easy, but I tell you this: whatever you feed, grows. If you feed the emotional side of you, nurturing old wounds, they will take on life. If you feed your spirit with the Word of God, it will be the dominant one. Nurture your spirit, not the soul. The soul of man is a beautiful thing when it is in its rightful place. The heart is beautiful when it is filled with God's love. When God's love in your spirit overflows to other parts of you, it will bring change in you and then change through you to others, even the ones who hurt you. Healing comes when love enters the scene.

We can't love in our own strength. In God's power is the only way. First He does the work in us and then because He is big picture–minded, He allows His love to spill out onto others. It is all about His timing and His way.

So we must get into agreement and alignment with God and His plans for all in our story.

Cross over your Jordan.

A NOTE TO THE READER

Embracing the Call

I HAVE NO MORE childhood memories to reflect on. I just have a few things left in my heart to share before our time together ends. I am forty-four years old, and I am just now embracing all God has for me—at least all I am aware of right now. Wherever you are on your journey to freedom, it is never too late for you. My pastor said this week from the pulpit, "If you have breath in your lungs and life in you, you still have a call to answer." I am embracing the call. Will you do this with me? You may think you don't have a call or a ministry, but if you have felt the desire to read this book, chances are you have a story of your own. And with your story, you will find there is your ministry. It is a ministry to pray for all involved in your story and to let God get glory from the painful things that have made you who you are today. We never want to erase the past, but be thankful for it and get all the profit God wants us to have from it. My roots are precious to me because they made me who I am today. Painful times are what made me call on the name of Jesus and know Him in a way I would never have known otherwise. I crossed over from Jordan to Canaan's land when I left religion and found relationship with the hero in my life, Jesus Christ—my redeemer, my travel companion on this journey, and my friend.

ABOUT THE AUTHOR

RENEE CARLISLE IS A wife of twenty-six years and a mother of two. She loves Jesus with all her, heart and she loves her family and friends. Her desire to see others walk in the freedom God longs to give is strong. She loves to encourage others in their walk with God and enjoys coffee dates with friends and time alone in the presence of God. She is passionate about discipleship in the local church body and freedom for the new believer in Christ. She is a motivational speaker and a lover and encourager of God and His Word.

CPSIA information can be obtained
at www.ICGtesting.com
Printed in the USA
FSHW01n0909261018
53306FS

9 781643 001081